SUPER AWESOME KIDS

A COLLECTION OF 25 SHORT INSPIRING STORIES OF AWESOME BOYS AND GIRLS ABOUT KINDNESS, GROWTH MINDSET, MINDFULNESS, CONFIDENCE AND COURAGE TO FULFIL THEIR TRUE POTENTIAL

MOTIVATIONAL BOOKS FOR CHILDREN 1

JOHN EBIBI

EBIBI BOOKS FOR KIDS

CONTENTS

Introduction   v

1. Mom's Virtues   1
2. Thabo And The Thembas   4
3. May And Stan's Partnership   6
4. Elkan, The Mayor   8
5. The Monk Test   10
6. Yemi's New School   13
7. Raju, The Persian Soldier   16
8. Abu, The Desert Champion   18
9. Dante, The Politician   20
10. Leonardo, The Soccer Wizard   22
11. Sly, The Gymnastics Queen   25
12. Sue, The Young Artist   28
13. Khulan, The Biologist   30
14. Saul's Lab Seeds   32
15. Beatriz, The Mindful Witch Doctor   34
16. Enuka, The Hyena Expert   37
17. Brian, Saves The Day   40
18. Philip And Caleb, The Maths Experts   42
19. Vincent In The Amazons   44
20. Speedy Lawrence   46
21. Sandip And The Pythons   49
22. Marcello In Soccer Trials   52
23. Miriam, The Contemporary Performer   54
24. Erika, The Humble Cheerleader   56
25. Fru, The Archery Champion   58
26. Final Thoughts   61
27. Ebibi Books For Kids Library   62

Copyright © 2022 by JOHN EBIBI All rights reserved. This book or any portion thereof may not be duplicated or utilized in any manner whatsoever without the express written permission of the publisher except for the use of brief quotations in a book review.

Legal Notice:

This book is copyright protected. This book is only for personal use. You cannot amend, distribute, sell, use, quote or paraphrase any part, or the content within this book, without the consent of the author or publisher.

Disclaimer Notice:

Please note that the information contained within this document is for educational and entertainment purposes only. All effort has been executed to present accurate, up-to-date, reliable, and complete information. No warranties of any kind are declared or implied. Readers acknowledge that the author is not engaging in the rendering of legal, financial, medical or professional advice. The content within this book has been derived from various sources. Please consult a licensed professional before attempting any techniques outlined in this book.

By reading this document, the reader agrees that under no circumstances is the author responsible for any losses, direct or indirect, which are incurred as a result of the use of the information contained within this document, including, but not limited to, — errors, omissions, or inaccuracies.

INTRODUCTION

To you, **Super Awesome Kid**.

You are blessed with many skills and talents, which you need to let shine through you so the world can see your true potential. You are exceptional in many ways, and you must remember that. Do not let the troubles of the world weigh down on your confidence, ambitions or goals because only you can walk your path, and the many friends and family you have, look up to you to become a star. Only you can flip the switch to make a difference, so do not let anyone take that away from you.

We live in a fast-paced and ever-changing world where situations can sometimes be challenging. When you work so hard, the results may not always go your way, your environment may be different, and you may have to adapt to a new setting. Regardless of what it is, your moment of brightness starts with your mindset, how you approach it with positivity to make a difference, and what you learn from it to be a better individual.

This book has several boys and girls just like you who have shown confidence and a positive mindset to achieve their dreams or overcome difficult situations. I share their experiences across five important social and interpersonal skills: kindness, growth mindset, mindfulness, confidence and courage. You can relate to their stories and learn from their experiences on how they navigated unique situations to become a much better individual and achieve your dream goals.

The book contains 25 short and impactful, inspiring stories of fantastic boys and girls drawn from different geographical settings and cultures. This is intended to give you exposure to different lifestyles and diverse experiences at an early age, to trigger your curiosity around various regions, and to build your diversity awareness and confidence.

It is essential to note that the purpose here is for you to enjoy the stories and apply whichever learnings relate to your specific circumstance to help you achieve your goals. Some other essential learnings embedded in this beautiful book include determination, the reward for kindness, the benefits of teamwork, resilience and lots more across a combination of fiction and non-fiction scenes.

I believe to be successful in our world today; these attributes are highly relevant for young kids like yourself to begin to get exposure to. You will also find an illustration with some of the stories. Feel free to color them to show your creativity and imagination to bring them to life. This way, you would be better immersed in the stories and key learnings, so you never forget them, even during the most challenging childhood situations.

I wish you a pleasant read and hope you are genuinely inspired, and that's because **You Are Super Awesome**!

John Ebibi

MOM'S VIRTUES

A long time ago, a sixty-year-old woman lived on the small Island of Mauritius, far off in the Indian Ocean, with her children, Yoshi and Suki. The lady had adopted them after their parents died in a car accident when they were only 2 and 3 years old. Yoshi was the older one and loved cooking for the family, which their mother loved so much.

They mostly had fish meals, given their abundance from the ocean. Suki enjoyed fishing with his friends and swimming in the sea at low tides. From time to time, the island residents would help one another and conduct fishing trips on boats for those unable to do so.

The people on the island loved their mom for her kindness as a teacher in her village. However, she would be retiring soon, which saddened many people.

Yoshi and Suki inherited the virtues of their mother, and they grew to be two strong and beautiful kids. The two were out on a boat fishing trip one day but had to cut short their fishing trip due to an ocean storm. So they were returning home with only two small fish for their dinner. On their way back, they saw a kid struggling for survival in the ocean and jumped in to rescue him. They brought him home as their mom would want.

Although the food was not enough, the family shared and gave the scared kid a blanket. Their mom put a word out in the village about the boy, and all villagers searched for his parents.

Later that night, a well-dressed lady came asking for the boy. It turns out the boy was the son of a famous, wealthy lady who lived at the hilltop estate of the village. The kindness of the family moved her so much that she offered to pay the tuition fees of Yoshi and Suki for them to further their education in college.

Their mother was proud of their kindness and encouraged them to practise it often because it was priceless.

THE END.

THABO AND THE THEMBAS

Long ago, a handyman called Themba lived in South Africa whose primary job was cutting grass using a lawn mower around his neighborhood. Themba had four well-educated kids who lived thousands of miles away in Europe. His wife had passed on earlier before all the kids had grown. Therefore, he was used to working hard to provide for himself and his family.

This particular year, he lost his job in the factory. As the country's young economy was not accommodating older individuals in the job market, he decided to be a handyman. Themba's friend Thabo loved his hard work ethic as he taught him many lessons on good virtues. Years passed, and Themba was much older and could no longer work.

One day, Thabo was seated at his office when his supervisor announced that they would plan for a charity event the following weekend to give back to the community. He was struck by the thought of Themba and other older people. In South Africa, it was uncommon for the elderly to grow old in nursing homes. After work, he walked to Themba to find him almost dying out of hunger.

Themba barely recognized him, and Thabo did not hesitate but carried him to his house and called the emergency services. The following day, Thabo had the perfect answer about the charity event for his boss - an event raising funds to help the elderly.

Later, Themba's children heard about their father and came to his rescue. Thabo's kindness touched the children. They committed to sponsoring the charity event and many future events which help the elderly in their local region of South Africa.

Thabo's kindness to Themba truly rewarded his work and community initiatives.

THE END.

MAY AND STAN'S PARTNERSHIP

The Mighty Justin bullied everyone in school, and no one dared to stand their ground whenever he attacked. He commanded everyone to call him Mighty, and even some teachers feared him because of his family's military background. May and Stan had just transferred into the school where May was in Justin's class, and Stan was one grade lower. In their former school, they did everything together and were great friends. May would attend high school the following year, and Stan felt sad.

On their first day of school, Justin made his presence known to the newly transferred student in his class, May, from whom he took all her lunch money. She was sad but asked around and heard that Stan would be the next victim. Therefore, she prepared Stan after school for his day.

The next day, Stan and May planned to lure Justin to the janitor's office, where the lighting was good. They had mounted a camera in the corner of the room, just in time for when Justin was looking for Stan after school. May directed him to the janitor's office.

Other students always wanted to witness such a scene, although no one dared to report him without enough evidence. They had their phone on live stream in readiness for any encounter with Justin. Stan, although scared, knew he would rely on May if things went wrong.

He provoked Justin by telling him to prove his worth. In the process, Justin felt disrespected and began boasting about all he had done to other students, including taking all lunch money for every new student.

Being live on camera, the Principal got a chance to watch it and had enough ground to expel The Mighty Justin for bullying. May and Stan's partnership and friendship worked in favor of all the bullied kids in the school. The pair were the newly popular and appreciated kids in the schoolyard.

THE END.

ELKAN, THE MAYOR

A long time ago, in Hawaii lived Nelly and Elkan, who were husband and wife. They raised their children to be respectful to others and work together as siblings. Nelly ran a food store in the market, supplied by their huge cash crop farm, while Elkan was an officer in the Mayor's office.

One day, the Mayor fell ill and passed away. He had to be replaced, and the most capable person who would handle their work was Elkan. He was reluctant to go ahead with the town's project since he knew the pressures of the office. A mysterious crop disease had hit their farmlands and devastated most of their harvest except Elkan and Nelly's since they used high-quality seedlings and unique farming methods.

Everyone was looking at Elkans' strategy after he became Mayor to save the town, and he desperately turned to Nelly and their elder children for advice. Elkan and his family agreed that they would supply their protected seedlings to all farmers in the town, so they would not miss out on the incoming rains.

A meeting of the Mayor and the farmer's community was also held. Nelly and their children provided training on the proper farming methods. They helped the farmers acquire the right amount of seedlings and fertilizers to ensure the best harvest results. The family helped out of kindness, friendship and love for the town.

After four months, their corn was ready for the first harvest, and the town obtained its highest yield, which was more than they could consume. So they had surplus requirements to export.

People gathered around, led by Elkan and his family, and used every means to transport their goods to other towns. No food was lost as the farmers earned more profits than any other year. They were grateful to Elkan and his family.

The teamwork demonstrated by Elkan saved the town from poverty, and the kindness of his family in sharing their success meant that the whole community benefited.

THE END.

THE MONK TEST

A long time ago, in Southeastern Asia, a young monk, Chun, was going through the stages of being accepted into the Pure Monk Society. At the time, he lived with his mother before the total commitment, where he would be taught many things about life.

However, his mother had taught Chun to cherish helping the society, especially offering help to those in need. Going to the monastery made his mother so happy. Many people came to that monastery because there were so many advantages that they would receive, including learning overseas and their families receiving allowances.

After coming of age, Chun set out for the mountain monastery. They were eight young men who hiked the hills on their way to the monastery since there was no vehicle access. On their way, they encountered a distressed child crying as they tried to calm her down.

Suddenly, the child started pointing at the rock. Her father, with whom they had come hiking, was trapped underneath a rock. The new monk boys had to decide whether to reach the monastery on time as instructed or help the man and his distressed daughter. This was a real test for the group since failure to arrive on time could lead to sanctions.

Six of the boys, led by Jules, opted to go to school and start their higher monk education. Chun and the youngest of the boys were left behind to help the man and the child. Time was running out, and it was only ten minutes to time, and they had not succeeded in helping the man.

Suddenly, the other six boys reappeared with sad faces as they walked past the two boys still struggling. It turns out the child and man requiring help were a test for the boys as part of the monk school assessment. Chun and the younger boy passed, and the others were sent back home.

Showing kindness is a work of mercy, according to the monastery, and should always be the first thing a human thinks about when people are suffering.

THE END.

YEMI'S NEW SCHOOL

Yemi woke up to find out her situation had not changed, it was only a dream, and she was still at her new school, far away from home in Abuja, Nigeria. After her parents got a job in the oil fields off the coast of Lagos, taking her with them was not an option because schools were not available seaside.

Yemi was forced to study in a boarding school, something entirely new to her. Like any other new student, adapting to boarding school was a challenge. It worsened when she realized she was expected to do her laundry without a laundry machine. The first month was devastating for her because her grades dropped, and she was neither performing well academically nor in extra-curricular activities.

Yemi almost gave up, until when the Principal announced that the best student that semester would earn a scholarship to study at Oxford University. It was the turning point for Yemi because she always wanted to study at Oxford like her Uncle Babatunde. She told her friend, Lanre, about getting the scholarship and her friend laughed at the idea.

Determined to win the prize, Yemi would wake up before everyone else to study. She even joined the school girls' football team. Her grades days after the big announcement did not improve significantly. Lanre appreciated her effort but told her not to push herself too hard by trying to be the best student because it was impossible. Yemi did not abandon her focus and joined the debate club to improve her communication and social skills.

Two weeks to the end of the semester, Yemi had still not led in a single assessment. Unfortunately, the Principal announced another student as the winner and not Yemi. However, later in the day, the Principal announced that they would be taking a runner-up student, the most improved student in all areas, and it was Yemi.

She was delighted and would not believe that she had achieved so much. The Principal cheered her to continue her determination to take action to develop herself and achieve her goal of attending Oxford University.

THE END.

RAJU, THE PERSIAN SOLDIER

Long ago, in the Persian Kingdom, a wonderful young lady named Raju, aged nine years, aspired to be a soldier. Raju loved hanging out with the boys because they played together, pretending to be soldiers defending their country.

However, the tradition in the region at the time was that police and military personnel were only selected from the male population, and the women would only provide service help and support to the front line.

The selections for the junior military academy usually occurred when they turned 12 years old. Raju was sad because she was not picked, and all her male friends joined the army. She wanted to change the system to include girls, which was unheard of in the Kingdom. She was not the first.

Instead of fighting directly, she decided to change her approach. Raju kept close contact with her friends in the military and borrowed their books to read. Since it was not against the military rules, they helped her. The boys did not know her plan but continued to help her with their books and assessments. Everyone was required to pass the curriculum before the physical training assessments.

On the assessment day, Raju showed up to take the test. She pleaded to the commander that she was capable and determined to join the military academy in whatever capacity. The commander accepted on the condition that she performed well.

Raju was successful and emerged with top-quartile performance. However, due to the law's restrictions, Raju could still not be granted a place as a frontline soldier. She was offered a position as an officer in the academy, an opportunity she was very excited about.

Her self-confidence and determination to grow within the academy showed how opportunities could still be created even when things didn't seem obvious. She quickly became a role model in the region and inspired many girls interested in joining the military academy.

THE END.

ABU, THE DESERT CHAMPION

*A*bu played with his dog, not noticing how the dust clouds were forming from the south of the desert. His brothers shouted at the top of their voices in their temporary shelter, and Abu saw the danger. The desert was near a village in Iran.

After the storm passed, they took their livestock home and continued studying in their thatched roofs houses. They lived with their mother, who worked as an attendant in a town hotel. Abu was motivated and always the first to get out of bed because he wanted to become a pilot and travel to Europe. He would get up early to watch the military helicopters fly over in the early morning hours. However, he could not attend school regularly as the country had a civil war, and most schools were frequently closed. Therefore,

Abu was focused and mindful daily of improving himself to have something to offer in case any opportunities came.

After two years of home studying, Abu was almost losing hope, but their school Principal, Hassan, heard of how he had remained focused for so long. For that reason, Hassan decided to do his best without making any promises to Abu. He applied to many schools in Europe and the United States of America. A year passed, and no one replied, and he gave up. Abu was still mindful of his life goal, and studying to be a pilot was part of that.

One Friday, after evening prayers, Abu received a letter from his Principal, Hassan, requesting a date for an assessment with Imperial College, London. It was overwhelming for him, but since he was determined to give his family a promising future, he prepared well and went for the evaluation. He passed the exams and was awarded a full scholarship for his program.

His family was proud of his achievement and cheered his determination to succeed. Abu's growth mindset gave him a fighting chance for a better life for himself and his family.

THE END.

DANTE, THE POLITICIAN

Dante woke up earlier than everyone to attend to their family's cattle livestock. He doubled as a farmer and an aspiring politician, although he was just 15 years old. Dante's father had given him a farm to run because he had great ambition. Dante was a student union president, although many did not appreciate high school politics. They were associated with a lack of discipline since it was used as a platform for spreading misinformation among students.

After assuming the president's office, Dante was confident he would change students' perspectives of the union. Moreover, Dante planned to seek support from local leaders to improve the school's reputation. After school, he would meet with his peer council members, and they organized to meet with the town Mayor to make important decisions about the school's funding.

On the day of the meeting, the most significant change was increasing the number of donations to schools by the local government. Everyone was waiting to see the outcome of the meeting, and so many people attended. Dante addressed the social hall, and people, including town residents, aired their views. The Mayor agreed to make changes in terms of adding the number of funds per semester.

Moreover, Dante's pitch moved the local community so much that the fundraising event was very successful. His self-confidence surprised the Mayor, who did not want to be left behind. He used his natural charm and charisma to influence politicians, and since the Mayor did not want to be outdone, he equally complied.

For that reason, he agreed to build more facilities in public schools around town, including the renovation of basketball pitches and the creation of swimming facilities.

Dante's self-confidence and growth mindset for his community made the headlines in his local town and newspapers, so much that, most town residents started joking about how he would be the next Mayor.

THE END.

LEONARDO, THE SOCCER WIZARD

*L*eonardo was born in Brazil and was the last of seven kids. The family's primary source of income was factory work for both his parents. Many people around the town knew Leonardo as the gentle giant because he was tall and well-built at nine years, and those that didn't know him well mistook him for an adult.

He was already in the town's football team and amongst the best at the district level. People loved him because he always helped his parents and supported them with the household work. Other children his age saw him as their leader because of his physical attributes and because he always helped where he could. Everyone knew that Leonardo would be successful in the future, given how focused and steadfast he was in everything he got involved in.

One day, Leonardo fell while playing and hurt his ankle.

With a hurt ankle, Leonardo felt like all his fears had come true since scouts from a Major League Soccer team in the United States would be visiting, and that was his opportunity to show his talent. However, he kept a calm head to focus on his recovery. The town doctor offered to help Leonardo recover and recommended various exercises he would take and food to eat before the tournament to accelerate his recovery.

Unfortunately for him, the team's coach would not include him in the team, regardless of the recovery, since he did not want Leonardo to be selected in place of his son, also in the team. It saddened many people in town, and the only way Leonardo would participate in the tournament was to play for a lower-ranking team. Leonardo was confident in his talent and potential and knew he only had one chance. His parents encouraged him that sometimes taking a step back by signing to a lower-ranking team to achieve his goal was not necessarily a wrong choice. What mattered more was how he shaped himself to grow further within the team.

Leonardo played well on the tournament day, earning his new team runners-up to the top spot. His standout performance also earned him the highest goal scorer award. As a result, Leonardo secured a junior team professional contract, enabling him to move to the United States with his family.

THE END.

SLY, THE GYMNASTICS QUEEN

Believing that her brother was gone would take time, and everyone would help but feel sorry for the young lady. Sly was an orphan and had lived with her elder brother since their parents died in a car accident when they were 9 and 17, respectively. Now, death had struck again, and she had no family to turn to.

Her brother worked hard so that child support would never show up at their doorstep to take his sister away. Things were happening fast, and the most worried person was her gymnastics coach. The Olympics were in three days, and they only had their chance of winning any medal if Sly participated.

Regardless, the whole gymnastics team did not go to training after hearing the tragic news and spent time comforting Sly before figuring out what was next.

She was told all the time she required healing, and the team left for the games without her knowledge.

The participants' names were announced a few hours before the opening performance. The coach and the other teammates were surprised to hear Sly's name called. Since it was a mistake and Sly would not be participating, the coach went to make the corrections and bumped into Sly as she was warming up. He was speechless, and Sly said she was determined to participate as her brother would have wished for.

The opening was excellent since Sly performed incredibly well, and no practice in the past went to waste. All the other teammates were so hyped and cheered her on. More importantly, they were more inspired to win despite not being tipped to be the favorites. However, they could not understand how Sly could keep her head up after losing her brother only two days earlier.

Sly tended to practice mindfulness and positive affirmations to focus on what was ahead of her. For instance, after the death of her parents, she was still at the top of her class the following month. Her brother had taught her always to keep calm and not let stress hinder every other aspect of her life. Sly did not want to let him down since he was gone. Mindfulness can be a great help in stressful moments. Sly's positive mindset amid adversity inspired her team to win.

THE END.

SUE, THE YOUNG ARTIST

The bell rang, and everyone ran to their respective duties, including Sue, the youngest of the recruits in the prestigious Japanese school. Her parents were busy on business trips, and the only way their child would stay near an adult was by leaving her in an art school in their neighborhood.

Although Sue loved art, it was not her choice to end up around a group of older girls and boys or to enter art school so soon. Regardless, Sue had to take the chance to improve her skills and learn what was necessary and required to stand out among other artists.

Her parents would return in a few days, so she did not have much pressure like the other girls who had to wait until the summer holiday, three months away, to see their parents.

Sue's happiness would only last two days since she was called into the Headteacher's office. "We are happy you will be staying with us until the end of the semester," The Headteacher said. That was music to him but a pain to Sue's ears.

Sue felt devastated, and everyone in the class would see it. Since she had not concentrated on making friends, it was even more difficult. After two days, Sue returned to the Headteacher and requested to add two more subjects besides art. If she was to stay until the summer holidays, she had to make the most of that time. She even embarked on making more friends so that they would help her learn Japanese since she was American.

Surprised by that turn of events, her teacher followed her progress in class closely. Sue made many friends and was loved by everyone in the classes she attended. Without her family close to her, she received immense aid to remain focused, adapt to the new environment and culture and learn every subject.

By the end of the semester, she did not just get a perfect score in art; she was top of her class. She kept her head up and was mindful of her circumstance, which ultimately paid off.

THE END.

KHULAN, THE BIOLOGIST

Khulan was a curious kid. At a very young age, she started dissecting small animals like frogs to find out about their internal organs and stitching injured rabbits using her mum's sewing kit. She was only ten years old and was already entrusted to check the biology and environmental labs in school.

Everyone loved her; most exhibitions contained her creativity, sometimes in ecological conservation. However, Khulan had one problem. Her brilliance would not matter in a few years because she was not in a great school, so she believed she would not utilize her potential. She was mindful of not dwelling on what she could not control as she was enjoying herself.

Since their town was located near a forest in Mongolia, tourists made lots of stops and were accommodated. To study the forests, a global environmental organization was looking for a qualified individual, aged between 10-16 years old, who knew about the forest and animals locally.

Most students submitted their qualifications, and as expected, those from prestigious schools were selected. Khulan's qualification was supported by the area chief recommending her to the organization. The six chosen for the interview were given a series of tests, and they all passed. Nevertheless, the final assessment was a practical test to assess their in-depth knowledge. This was a walk in the park for Khulan, as she went further to recommend the organization to use her research in the biology and environmental labs at her school.

At this point, the examiners were impressed and saw no point in interviewing the rest of the candidates because Khulan had demonstrated passion, talent, and practical ability. It was going to be a mutual relationship as they would be learning from her, and she would be learning from them.

"This is pure talent," the organization's CEO said after reading Khulan's evaluation as she was offered the job.

THE END.

SAUL'S LAB SEEDS

The relief food line was getting longer every day, and people had become meaner to one another than ever.

"This is the result of environmental degradation," Saul cried on how desperate people had become.

He was a high school teacher in Bangladesh who headed the food security shortage initiative. He was mandated to distribute government-provided relief food around his community by the area's local leaders after the famine had hit Asia severely.

Travelling was difficult because they were experiencing scorching days due to global warming, and at night it was dangerous because people were desperate and had turned to robbery. Saul had been working on several solutions for his town, like a seed requiring less water and was resistant to disease and pest attacks. The seed was introduced to the local government, but it failed the test and ended up even worse than the ordinary seedlings.

One day, as Saul was giving out relief food in his office at school, he came across a man that had been following his research on the perfect foods. The man was a marine biologist and said he could help. Saul said it was a waste of time because the council would not support him.

However, mindful of the famine impact, he accepted the input of the marine biologist, and he adjusted his research to explore other solutions which could benefit his community. Upon carrying the test himself, the crops survived and with good yields. He shared his latest updated findings with the food security board, and the members appreciated his efforts.

The seed was approved, and Saul's resilience and mindfulness of his community impact gave him a hero's treatment around Bangladesh.

THE END.

BEATRIZ, THE MINDFUL WITCH DOCTOR

*L*ong ago in Venezuela, there lived a family believed to be in the long lineage of witches. For that reason, many persecuted them and did not always accept anyone associated with them into their social circles. Children born from this lineage suffered something they did not know its origin, and soon, people began rejecting marriage proposals from anyone from that family.

Beatriz was the last child associated with this family, and the family decided to take her to the United States to protect her from her villagers. In the US, Beatriz was brilliant and studied medicine in college. She had the urge to research her background back home and first ensured she had accumulated a lot of capital. However, she had no idea that her family was hated back home.

Beatriz was made aware of the situation and what to expect. She was devastated for a few days but decided to proceed with her plan. Her village was deficient in a health centre, and Beatriz erected one which would not charge a consultation fee for the locals. Regardless, the villagers were reluctant to use those services and saw them as a trap for witchcraft, as they referred to her as the witch doctor.

One day, a villager was sick and on the verge of dying, and the only help was in Beatriz's hospital. He was taken to that hospital, treated for two days, and discharged. Nothing superstitious happened to him, and every villager who criticized Beatriz's family was ashamed.

They began going to Beatriz's family to apologize, and their long-lived persecution slowly ended. Beatriz's mindfulness enabled her to face the detractors of her family by doing well and not allowing their sentiments to affect the goodwill of her family and community.

THE END.

ENUKA, THE HYENA EXPERT

Everything that happened that day made Femi think twice about how he would handle his people throughout the night. Femi was an army captain who led a peacekeeping mission in Chad, a war-torn country in Central Africa. His unit was mandated with rescuing the rest of his team, and they remained tasked with making it to an open field to board their plane home.

However, the rebels used wild animals to attack the peacekeeping group. They released a well-trained group of hyenas which attacked the group and killed most of their soldiers. This was an unexpected move. Femi was impressed and terrified because dealing with wild animals was not his strength. The remaining members of his team were getting restless when a young boy entered the camp.

Femi was surprised because he crept in unnoticed. His name was Enuka from Borno State, in Northern Nigeria. His father was among the area leaders killed, and he was willing to help them escape the group of rebels. Enuka had a local medicinal formula that would paralyze the hyenas and enable Femi and his team to make it to the plane without further attacks.

Femi accepted reluctantly as Enuka proceeded before the soldiers into the hostile enemy position, which had the hyenas. He applied his medicinal formula along the known paths and returned without attack. The team stayed back and watched as the pace of the oncoming hyenas slowed down as the formula affected their breathing and internal organs. They all laid down helpless.

Everyone in the camp was challenged by Enuka's self-confidence and how he could effectively control hyenas. The team became more motivated to work for what was right. His self-belief and confidence had impressed many officers.

Later, Enuka would be invited to join the United Nations Peace Keeping Mission as news of what he did had spread fast, and they were keen to learn from his expertise and apply it in other regions.

THE END.

BRIAN, SAVES THE DAY

Brian was born in a family of seven in Ireland, and as the sixth child, he didn't get much attention. Although he went to a good school, education was not his stronghold. However, Brian did not give up because he had to balance academic and extra-curricular activities.

Brian concentrated in both areas, although he was not the best. His elder brothers joked about how he wanted to achieve everything and seemed to be failing. But his organization and resilience in class and outdoors pleased his school Principal. The Principal rewarded him with a library card for the newly opened library in town, although his siblings found it funny because his grades were below average.

With one year remaining, Brian increased the intensity of participation in both basketball and education and was improving in both. His parents were supportive, although they found basketball a waste of time. Nonetheless, since they focused on their youngest son and eldest daughter, who was getting married, they did not pay much attention to Brian's improvements.

With the basketball tournament nearing, the coach was desperate to make a good team, and Brian was chosen to be part of the team. After school, Brian would remain at the court and practice intensively. His resilience to take more practice hours amazed the coach. However, he was unused for most of the games.

In the tournament's final match, the team was losing, and Brian came in as a substitute to support the team effort. Brian's new skills learned in self-practice helped them win the season's final game and saved the day for his team. His coach and team peers were impressed with his performance which earned him a regular starting position for the next season.

His resilience and confidence to try new things on the field and in class were being rewarded and paying off.

THE END.

PHILIP AND CALEB, THE MATHS EXPERTS

"hilip and Caleb, you will work on your coding project together."

The maths teacher had instructed the students to work in pairs to develop some maths applications, which were challenging for many people. Philip and Caleb were two friends that never left each other in anything, and the maths teacher did not attempt to separate them.

However, Peter and Pius, the twins, were always leading the class in almost everything, and students thought it was unfair for them to be chosen in the same group. Philip and Caleb were average students and had no chance in a head-to-head oral test against the twins. It was not difficult for Philip and Caleb to agree on the application since they had almost similar interests.

They chose to code and decided to create a simple application. They allocated about two hours every day to work on their project. The boys were very nervous about the proposal day as the best project would be showcased at the New York Maths Exhibitions.

Philip and Caleb were the last to present their project. And so far, no group had impressed the teacher, but the twins' project was the best of all shown so far. They were confident they would emerge winners and even dared to make fun of Philip and Caleb's input to their coding project.

Nonetheless, the pair were confident because they had made a practical code that would be used to follow live classes using the class social media groups. The project took the class by surprise, and the teacher had to cross-check their input with a computer expert in the school. Regardless, she was convinced they came up with the project because the two were always cooperative in other assessments.

Their coding project was shortlisted for its simplicity and relevance. They would attend the New York exhibition, but before that, they became famous throughout the whole school. The other kids believed they could do the same if Philip and Caleb did better than the twins. They were all inspired, felt anything was possible if they worked hard, and remained confident in their abilities.

THE END.

VINCENT IN THE AMAZONS

Vincent waited long for his son to return from their school trip, but there were no signs of any vehicle using that road. He was beginning to worry about what might have happened to a bus full of children.

Nightfall was approaching, and parents had begun asking questions. The local news station had already started reporting about the loss of children in the Amazon. News reached the parents that they were on their way, and all parents ran in that direction. However, Vincent's son Jeremy was absent. The bus had delayed searching for them in the jungle.

Vincent was so worked up by the news that he stormed out of the Principal's office and couldn't understand how that was possible. He knew this was not the time to lay blame but to think of the best solution to find Jeremy.

Vincent packed a bag of food supplies and set out to find his son. Jeremy was lost in the Amazon forest with bears, leopards, and antelopes. Helped by some volunteers, they entered the forest and retraced all the points visited by the whole class and still did not find the boy.

One day passed, and all the other parents were exhausted by the search. Vincent would not give up because Jeremy was his only son. He continued for two more days and ran out of food supplies. He was getting deeper into the Amazon, which had not been explored, so he was increasingly worried.

As Vincent was preparing to continue the search after a long rest, they were captured by a group of weird-looking men from a tribe in the forest. They had rescued Jeremy.

Vincent and the team were thrilled to have found Jeremy as they sent signals for rescue. The tribe members accommodated them for another day as they waited to leave using a safer route.

Vincent's determination and belief recovered his son, and he couldn't be happier to have found Jeremy safe and sound.

THE END.

SPEEDY LAWRENCE

*L*awrence was born in New Zealand and started schooling aged 5, as the country's school regulations instructed. However, most people did not believe his age as time went by because he was pretty small compared to his peers.

The school always participated in rugby tournaments, and Lawrence's dream was to compete in the game and play professionally for his country. As time passed, he was later diagnosed with a growth disability in fourth grade. This meant that he would not grow any taller. He was already below average in height, which devastated him because he felt he would be at a disadvantage in the selection of any competitive rugby team.

However, Lawrence had one strength, he was swift and speedy naturally and decided to use that to his advantage.

Since Lawrence was aware he would not grow any taller, he joined the school team in fourth grade, while most people joined in sixth grade.

At first, the coach thought Lawrence was with the school's journalism club to report on the team's progress. Practice sessions took place four days a week, and he attended all of them for a whole month without being allowed to play in a competitive game. Regardless, Lawrence was determined to prove himself and confident in his ability.

Fortunately, that coach retired, and a new coach, Evans, was brought in. Lawrence did not stop working hard with determination to please the incoming head coach and be selected for the team. He had to endure mockery from his teammates, who were convinced the new coach would rely on the selection of the retired one.

After watching the team in training, to everyone's surprise, he picked Lawrence as a key member of his squad to leverage his skills and pace. Coach Evans did not rely so much on the former coach's notes, and Lawrence retained that position until he graduated and immensely contributed to the team's success.

Lawrence was delighted that his resilience in training and determination to succeed had paid off.

THE END.

SANDIP AND THE PYTHONS

Getting close to the Spike Forest in Cambodia was unheard off because of the many disappearances. For that reason, parents warned their children about grazing their goats near the edge of the forests.

People created many false stories about the forest and why it was dangerous to scare away children whenever they wanted them to behave in the right way. Nonetheless, the stories were not far from the truth because a large family of pythons had infested the forest and multiplied. Cattle and people were attacked and killed if they went deeper into the forest. And the local government was working on controlling the breeding of the reptiles.

One summer day, a helicopter ferrying children on a science trip made an emergency landing in the area.

Sandip, a girl from a village near the Spike Python Forest, saw what happened and immediately called the area chief. Before she organized a search party, she rushed into the forest. Still, she was late because she found a pair of giant pythons surrounding the terrified children whose pilot and teacher were already unconscious from the landing.

Suddenly, a loud noise of branches cracking was heard, and the children thought it was a rescue party. It turned out that the pair of pythons had more company joining them, as they had humans to prey on. Sandip knew she had to take her chances with a dozen pythons getting closer to the children.

She began attacking them with a bow and arrow to disperse them. This caused them to retreat, allowing Sandip to access and administer some first aid to the teacher and pilot first. Minutes later, the pilot triggered the emergency alarm, a loud sound and lots of smoke that caused the pythons to retreat further, enabling access for more support before the pythons could ever regroup.

A tragic story would be told if not for Sandip's courage to take on the pythons all by herself to save the kids' lives. The rescue mission was completed. All the kids returned to their families feeling grateful and inspired to step up and use their strengths when needed.

THE END.

MARCELLO IN SOCCER TRIALS

Marcello grew up in Italy and was scared because his family would be relocating to England since a global company offered his mother, a job in London. Unsure of how long she would be working there, she had to carry her son since she was a single mother.

Marcello was a great soccer player back in Italy, and teams like AC Milan were already scouting for him. Upon relocating to London, he had to prove himself again. The biggest challenge was learning English, which prompted him to enter an English class if he was going to join an English soccer academy. His mother paid for home tutoring for two months for a better start, delaying his trials for the 9-year-old at Chelsea Football Club, one of the prestigious academies in the City of London. Marcello was a huge talent back in Milan but was scared to do trials with 12-year-olds.

On the trial day, Marcello sang a favorite song taught by his father, a legendary soccer player. He sang to hype himself so that he would gain courage. However, the older boys laughed at him since he was small and would use him as a reference, saying he was a joke to the soccer fraternity.

Marcello was about to withdraw, but his mother told him that his father was watching him from heaven. She also reminded him that he was the best back in Italy. He, therefore, garnered courage and went to trials well-charged.

Marcello played so well that the coach thought he was amongst the 12-year-olds. The following day, he made the headlines on the club's newspaper front page with the headline, "The Italian Wizzard Is Back", following the success of previous Italians at the club.

From that experience, Marcello knew he needed courage as much as his talent to remain focused on his goals and succeed in his new club regardless of the language barrier or peer pressures.

THE END.

MIRIAM, THE CONTEMPORARY PERFORMER

Miriam was born the only girl in a family of six in Malawi, East Africa and had to struggle and fight with the boys for attention and most things. She also got used to the games played by the boys and their friends, and since most girls were older in the village, Miriam did not have many options.

Together with the boys, they got into dancing and promised each other they would dance professionally when they became adults. Nevertheless, her tribe did not allow her to continue moving with the boys when she reached nine years old because she was supposed to go through initiation (a common practice in preparing young girls for adulthood).

Still, since Miriam was on the girls' team, the boys would practice their routines together while Miriam was learning what society expected of her. From the initiation, Miriam was expected to help with house chores and become a mother one day. Regardless, she had been telling her family about dancing, and they did not like it.

After the three months initiation, the boys' group was already way ahead of Miriam in dancing, and they were even aware that culture would hinder her from being in the group. However, Miriam was not convinced that her dancing dream would vanish because others said so.

Days later, a competition was announced in town where people showcased their talents. Everyone in the boys' group thought letting Miriam in at that time was too late, and she would be a liability. Therefore, she was left out of the group. However, she did not give up; hence continued resiliently practising and gathered the courage to participate individually. Of course, no one expected her to show up dancing in the competition, and her parents were convinced that they had killed her dream.

On D-day, she performed last and had a stand-out performance. The boys' group couldn't believe how good Miriam was, while her parents had a mixture of excitement and shock. Miriam's resilience in practising her dance and the courage to participate alone gave her a fighting chance to showcase her hidden talent to the community.

THE END.

ERIKA, THE HUMBLE CHEERLEADER

Upon reaching home, her brothers and sisters were asleep, and no one had given Pius, the street beggar, any food. They either forgot or saw it as less important. Erika was the cheerleaders' captain and had inspired her team to be the best in the county. Everyone would expect that she was mean, beautiful, and a bully to kids at school. She was the opposite, which is probably why her team was so disciplined.

Nevertheless, that would not last because Emily, the new student and the daughter of the largest donor to the school, had just joined the cheerleading team. Weak individuals who wanted to be her friend supported her in ejecting Erika as the captain, and they succeeded. Even though the title was with Emily, teachers and the coach continuously saw Erika's charisma. Finally, Emily became jealous of Erika's effortless influence in school and plotted to eject her from the group. The group had now become political, and Erika was ejected.

Erika was devastated the first two weeks because her dream of being a cheerleader in college was snatched away. She had to devise a comeback if she was to have a chance in college at cheerleading. Her class tutor advised her to enter the charity group, giving her a good idea. There was no rule against creating another cheerleading team.

Erika based her cheerleading team on charity which began by helping beggars around the neighborhoods. Regardless, Emily still attacked the new cheerleading group, and the Principal asked Emily to spare herself the trauma, as Erika decided to remain focused on her group.

The only way to maintain peace in school was to devise a way to eliminate one or merge the groups. Both groups preferred the former and went head to head on a show. Erika's team emerged successful, and her volunteering efforts were a bonus. Although Erika was humble, she did not allow others to push her around. Her courage was top-notch, and her charity work allowed others to experience her excellence. She was still open to Emily joining her so they had a unified front for the school.

THE END.

FRU, THE ARCHERY CHAMPION

Once upon a time, a young boy named Fru lived in a small village called Baba. Fru was the eldest of seven children and often spent time with his father hunting after school. He would do what his parents told him, making them very happy and proud of him.

Sometimes, Fru would visit his friend Fon, and Fon's parents enjoyed his company as much as Fru's parents did there. Almost everyone in the neighborhood knew Fru for how obedient he was. Most importantly, he was known for being very good at archery. He would beat all his peers at the game and be named "The Godson of Baba Archery."

Hunting was a means of livelihood in the village, so archery was often encouraged to get young children to learn the skill.

One day, the town Mayor organized an archery tournament; where children from different villages would come together to play against each other. Fru was excited about the challenge but was also very scared. He had never played against anyone he didn't know, let alone children older than him. Worst still, every other champion from the other villages were older children who would beat Fru at the game.

The day of the tournament came, Fru was still scared that he even asked the Chief if he could be allowed not to play and instead watch. But his entire village was hoping he would win the championship trophy for himself and the village's glory. The other boys and girls looked at how little Fru was, and they laughed, knowing they would win.

Fru gathered enough courage to play the first round, the second, and the third. He won each game by very high margins. He was finally announced and awarded the trophy for being the champion.

He was courageous enough to take up the challenge, which he did and won, making his entire village proud of him. Fru learnt never to doubt himself, regardless of who his opponent was.

THE END.

If you found this storybook helpful or inspiring, please spare me two minutes of your valuable time to leave me an honest review on my Amazon page on how your child found this book. Were they inspired? What thoughts were triggered as they went through the different stories?
I look forward to hear your thoughts.
Many thanks

lease check out my other books for kids available on Amazon:

- Awesome Princesses, Mermaids & Unicorns Coloring Book For Kids
- Amazing Dinosaur Alphabet Coloring Book For Kids
- The Cutest Pet Animals Coloring Book For Kids
- Never Stop Believing: 25 Inspiring Short Stories Of Amazing Girls On Growth Mindset, Teamwork, Friendship, Self Confidence And Determination

www.ingramcontent.com/pod-product-compliance
Lightning Source LLC
Chambersburg PA
CBHW040242130526
44590CB00049B/4177